Octaves for the Cello

Book Three

by Cassia Harvey

CHP140

www.charveypublications.com

D to High A

Cassia Harvey

Lavender's Blue

Traditional, arr. Harvey

D to C♯, and High A

Musette

Leclair, arr. Harvey

High A Hand Position in A major

Brandenburg Concerto

Bach, arr. Harvey

Shifting to High A from D

Hungarian Dance

Kajoni Codex, arr. Harvey

5

Shifting to High A from D with a scale

Greenland Fisheries

Traditional, arr. Harvey

6

Shifting to E from the D octave

The Riddle Song

Traditional, arr. Harvey

7

Shifting to E from the D octave

Suo-Gan

Traditional, arr. Harvey

8

Shifting to F♯ from the D octave

Early One Morning

Traditional, arr. Harvey

9

Shifting to G and G♯ from the D octave

Dalby Ram

Traditional, arr. Harvey

Prelude

Bach, arr. Harvey

10

D to High A in C major

Gavotte

Handel, arr. Harvey

Shifting to High A from Low A

Bourree

Bach, arr. Harvey

12   Shifting from Low A to High A in A minor

Sonata

Cimarosa, arr. Harvey

13

A to High A in D minor

Concerto

Tartini, arr. Harvey

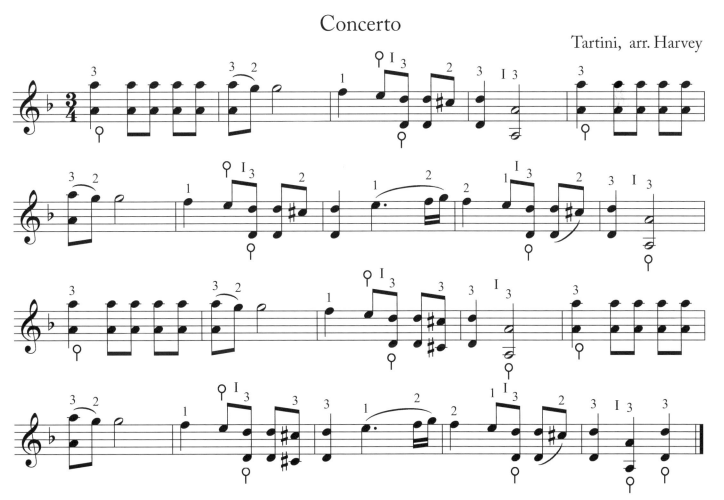

A to B and High A

Allegro

L. Mozart, arr. Harvey

15

A to D to High A

Allegro

Rameau, arr. Harvey

Shifting to E and A from the A octave

Sonata

J. Schobert, arr. Harvey

17

A to High A with Scales

Sonata

Kozeluch, arr. Harvey

18

A and D to High A

Soldier, Will You Marry Me?

Traditional, arr. Harvey

19

A and D to High A

Theme from Flute Concerto #2

Mozart, arr. Harvey

A and D to High A

Theme from Violin Concerto #4

Mozart, arr. Harvey

B to High A

The Girl with the Flaxen Hair

Debussy, arr. Harvey

B to High A

Minuet

Bach, arr. Harvey

23

B to E

Minuet

Bach, arr. Harvey

24

B to F♯ and G♯

Turkish Rondo

Herz, arr. Harvey

B to High A

25

Vivace

Handel, arr. Harvey

C# to High A

Gymnopedie

Satie, arr. Harvey

27

C♯ to High A

Andulko

Traditional, arr. Harvey

C♯ to High A

Hungarian Dance

Stark Virginal Book, arr. Harvey

29

C# to High A via E

Theme from Horn Concerto #4

Mozart, arr. Harvey

30

A, B, C♯, and D to High A

O Mio Babbino Caro

Puccini, arr. Harvey

Thumb Position Studies for the Cello
1

Book Three: Moving Around

Cassia Harvey

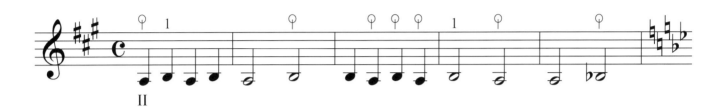

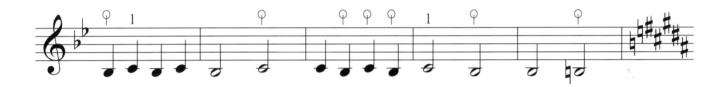

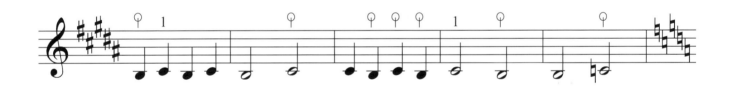

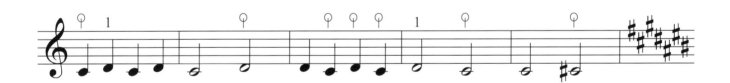

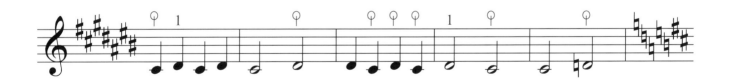